W9-BVC-659

Norms for the Distribution and Reception of Holy Communion Under Both Kinds in the Dioceses of the United States of America

LITURGY DOCUMENTARY SERIES 13

United States Conference of Catholic Bishops • Washington, D.C.

The document *Norms for the Distribution and Reception of Holy Communion Under Both Kinds in the Dioceses of the United States of America* was developed by the Bishops' Committee on the Liturgy of the United States Conference of Catholic Bishops (USCCB). It was approved by the full body of U.S. Catholic bishops at its June 2001 General Meeting, received the subsequent *recognitio* of the Holy See, and has been authorized for publication by the undersigned.

—Monsignor William P. Fay
General Secretary, USCCB

CONTENTS

CONGREGATION FOR DIVINE WORSHIP AND
THE DISCIPLINE OF THE SACRAMENTS

Prot. 1383/01/L

THE UNITED STATES OF AMERICA

In response to the request of His Excellency, the Most Reverend Joseph Fiorenza, Bishop of Galveston-Houston, President of the Conference of Bishops of the United States of America, made in a letter dated June 21, 2001, and by virtue of the faculties granted to this Congregation by the Supreme Pontiff JOHN PAUL II, we grant recognition of the text entitled, "Norms for the Distribution and Reception of Holy Communion under Both Kinds in the Dioceses of the United States of America," as found in the attached copy, and which shall be inserted into future editions of the Roman Missal published in English for use in the dioceses of the same Conference.

Mention of the recognition granted by this Congregation must be included in the published text of these norms.

All things to the contrary notwithstanding.

From the Congregation for Divine Worship and the Discipline of the Sacraments, March 22, 2002.

✠ Jorge A. Cardinal Medina Estevez
Prefect

✠ Francesco Pio Tamburrino
Archbishop-Secretary

v

UNITED STATES CONFERENCE OF CATHOLIC BISHOPS
UNITED STATES OF AMERICA

DECREE

On June 15, 2001, the Latin members of the United States Conference of Catholic Bishops approved the attached "Norms for the Distribution and Reception of Holy Communion under Both Kinds in the Dioceses of the United States of America."

In accord with the approval of these norms and following the confirmation of this action by the Congregation for Divine Worship and the Discipline of the Sacraments on March 22, 2002 (Prot. 1383/01/L), they are hereby published as particular law for all Latin celebrations of the Sacred Liturgy in the dioceses of the United States of America.

The effective date of this decree will be April 7, 2002, the Second Sunday of Easter.

Given at the General Secretariat of the United States Conference of Catholic Bishops, Washington, D.C. on March 28, 2002, Holy Thursday.

Most Reverend Wilton D. Gregory
Bishop of Belleville
President, United States Conference of Catholic Bishops

Reverend Monsignor William P. Fay
General Secretary

CONGREGATION FOR DIVINE WORSHIP AND THE DISCIPLINE OF THE SACRAMENTS

Prot. 1382/01/L

THE UNITED STATES OF AMERICA

In response to the request of His Excellency, the Most Reverend Joseph Fiorenza, Bishop of Galveston-Houston, President of the Conference of Bishops of the United States of America, made in a letter dated June 21, 2001, and in virtue of the faculties granted to this Congregation by the Supreme Pontiff, JOHN PAUL II, we grant that in the dioceses of this same Conference, for grave pastoral reasons, the faculty may be given by the diocesan Bishop to the priest celebrant to use the assistance, when necessary, even of extraordinary ministers in the cleansing of sacred vessels after the distribution of Communion has been completed in the celebration of Mass. This faculty is conceded for a period of three years as a dispensation from the norm of the *Institutio Generalis, edito typica tertia* of the Roman Missal.

All things to the contrary notwithstanding.

From the Congregation for Divine Worship and the Discipline of the Sacraments, March 22, 2002.

✠ Jorge A. Cardinal Medina Estevez
Prefect

✠ Francesco Pio Tamburrino
Archbishop-Secretary

UNITED STATES CONFERENCE OF CATHOLIC BISHOPS
UNITED STATES OF AMERICA

DECREE

On June 15, 2001, the Latin members of the United States Conference of Catholic Bishops approved a request for an indult from the prescriptions of the *Institutio Generalis Missalis Romani, editio typica tertia*, allowing for the purification of sacred vessels by extraordinary ministers of Holy Communion when deemed pastorally appropriate by the diocesan bishop.

In a decree dated March 22, 2002 (Prot. 1383/01/L), the Congregation for Divine Worship and the Discipline of the Sacraments granted an indult whereby, for grave pastoral reasons, the diocesan Bishop may grant to priest celebrants the faculty to permit extraordinary ministers of Holy Communion to assist with the purification of sacred vessels after the distribution of Communion at Mass. This faculty dispenses from the norm of the *Institutio Generalis Missalis Romani, editio typica tertia* for a period of three years.

The indult is hereby published and is effective immediately.

Given at the General Secretariat of the United States Conference of Catholic Bishops, Washington, D.C. on March 28, 2002, Holy Thursday.

Most Reverend Wilton D. Gregory
Bishop of Belleville
President, United States Conference of Catholic Bishops

Reverend Monsignor William P. Fay
General Secretary

PART I
Holy Communion:
The Body and Blood of
the Lord Jesus

The Mystery of the Holy Eucharist

1. On the night before he died, Christ gathered his Apostles in the upper room to celebrate the Last Supper and to give us the inestimable gift of his Body and Blood. "He did this in order to perpetuate the sacrifice of the Cross throughout the centuries until He should come again, and so to entrust to His beloved spouse, the Church, a memorial of His death and resurrection. . . ."[1] Thus, in the Eucharistic Liturgy we are joined with Christ on the altar of the cross and at the table of the upper room in "the sacrificial memorial in which the sacrifice of the cross is perpetuated and [in] the sacred banquet of communion with the Lord's body and blood."[2]

2. Like all acts of the sacred Liturgy, the Eucharist uses signs to convey sacred realities. *Sacrosanctum Concilium: Constitution on the Sacred Liturgy* reminds us that "the sanctification of man is manifested by signs perceptible to the senses, and is effected in a way which is proper to each of these signs."[3] In a preeminent way the Eucharistic Liturgy

---

1   Second Vatican Council, *Sacrosanctum Concilium: Constitution on the Sacred Liturgy* [SC] (December 4, 1963), no. 47. (All Vatican II citations here refer to the following edition: Walter M. Abbott, ed., *The Documents of Vatican II* [New York: Guild Press, 1966].)

2   United States Catholic Conference–Libreria Editrice Vaticana, *Catechism of the Catholic Church* [CCC] (2000), no. 1382.

3   SC, no. 7.

uses the signs of bread and wine in obedience to the Lord's command and after their transformation gives them to us as the Body and Blood of Christ in the act of communion. It is by taking and sharing the Eucharistic bread and chalice—"signs perceptible to the senses"—that we obey the Lord's command and grow in the likeness of the Lord whose Body and Blood they both signify and contain.

3. The Eucharist constitutes "the Church's entire spiritual wealth, that is, Christ Himself, our Passover and living bread."[4] It is the "sacrament of sacraments."[5] Through it "the work of our redemption is accomplished."[6] He who is the "living bread that came down from heaven" (Jn 6:51) assures us, "Whoever eats my flesh and drinks my blood has eternal life, and I will raise him on the last day. For my flesh is true food, and my blood is true drink" (Jn 6:54-55).

4. The eyes of faith enable the believer to recognize the ineffable depths of the mystery that is the Holy Eucharist. The *Catechism of the Catholic Church* offers us a number of images from our tradition to refer to this most sacred reality: Eucharistic assembly (synaxis), action of thanksgiving, breaking of the bread, memorial, holy sacrifice, Lord's Supper, holy and divine Liturgy, Holy Communion, and Holy Mass.[7] The Eucharistic species of bread and wine derive from the work of human hands. In the action of the Eucharist this bread and this wine are transformed and become our spiritual food and drink. It is Christ, the true vine, who gives life to the branches (cf. Jn 15:1-6). As bread from heaven (cf. Jn 6:41), bread of angels, the chalice of salvation, and

---

4   Second Vatican Council, *Presbyterorum Ordinis: Decree on the Ministry and Life of Priests* [PO] (December 7, 1965), no. 5.

5   Congregation for Divine Worship and the Discipline of the Sacraments, *General Instruction of the Roman Missal* [GIRM] (2000), no. 368.

6   *Sacramentary*, Prayer Over the Gifts, Evening Mass of the Lord's Supper, p. 138.

7   CCC, nos. 1328-1332.

the medicine of immortality,[8] the Eucharist is the promise of eternal life to all who eat and drink it (cf. Jn 6:50-51). The Eucharist is a sacred meal, "a sacrament of love, a sign of unity, a bond of charity"[9] in which Christ calls us as his friends to share in the banquet of the kingdom of heaven (cf. Jn 15:15). This bread and chalice were given to his disciples at the Last Supper. This spiritual food has been the daily bread and sustenance for his disciples throughout the ages. The bread and wine of the Lord's Supper—his Body and Blood—as broken and poured out constitute the irreplaceable food for the journey of the "pilgrim church on earth."[10] The Eucharist perpetuates the sacrifice of Christ, offered once and for all for us and for our salvation, making present the victory and triumph of Christ's death and resurrection.[11] It is strength for those who journey in hope through this life and who desire to dwell with God in the life to come. Our final sharing in the Eucharist is *viaticum*, the food for the final journey of the believer to heaven itself. Through these many images, the Church helps us to see the Eucharist as union with Christ from whom she came, through whom she lives, and towards whom she directs her life.[12]

Holy Communion
5. While the heart of the celebration of the Eucharist is the Eucharistic Prayer, the consummation of the Mass is found in Holy Communion, whereby the people purchased for the Father by his beloved Son eat and drink the Body and Blood of Christ. They are thereby joined together as members of Christ's mystical Body, sharing the one life of the Spirit. In the great sacrament of the altar, they are joined to Christ Jesus and to one another.

---

8   Cf. St. Ignatius of Antioch, *Ad. Eph.*, 20, 2.

9   SC, no. 47.

10   *Sacramentary*, Eucharistic Prayer III, p. 554.

11   SC, no. 6.

12   Cf. Second Vatican Council, *Lumen Gentium: Dogmatic Constitution on the Church* (November 21, 1964), no. 3.

It was also Christ's will that this sacrament be received as the soul's spiritual food to sustain and build up those who live with his life, as he said, "He who eats me, he also shall live because of me" (Jn 6:57). This sacrament is also to be a remedy to free us from our daily defects and to keep us from mortal sin. It was Christ's will, moreover, that this sacrament be a pledge of our future glory and our everlasting happiness and, likewise, a symbol of that one body of which he is the head (cf. Lk 22:19 and 1 Cor 11:3). He willed that we, as members of this body should be united to it by firm bonds of faith, hope and love, so that we might all say the same thing, and that there might be no dissensions among us (cf. 1 Cor 1:10).[13]

As Catholics, we fully participate in the celebration of the Eucharist when we receive Holy Communion. We are encouraged to receive Communion devoutly and frequently. In order to be properly disposed to receive Communion, participants should not be conscious of grave sin and normally should have fasted for one hour. A person who is conscious of grave sin is not to receive the Body and Blood of the Lord without prior sacramental confession except for a grave reason where there is no opportunity for confession. In this case, the person is to be mindful of the obligation to make an act of perfect contrition, including the intention of confessing as soon as possible (canon 916). A frequent reception of the Sacrament of Penance is encouraged for all.[14]

---

13 Council of Trent, Session xiii (October 11, 1551), *De ratione institutionis ss. huius sacramenti*. (Latin text in Henricus Denzinger and Adolfus Schönmetzer, eds., *Enchiridion Symbolorum: Definitionum et Declarationum de Rebus Fidei et Morum* [DS] [Barcinone: Herder, 1976], 1638. English text in John F. Clarkson et al., *The Church Teaches* [TCT] [St. Louis, Mo.: B. Herder, 1955], 720.)

14 National Conference of Catholic Bishops, *Guidelines for the Reception of Communion* (Washington, D.C., 1996).

Union with Christ

6. The Lord himself gave us the Eucharist at the Last Supper. The Eucharistic sacrifice "is wholly directed toward the intimate union of the faithful with Christ through communion."[15] It is Christ himself who is received in Holy Communion, who said to his disciples, "Take and eat, this is my body." Giving thanks, he then took the chalice and said: "Take and drink, this is the cup of my blood. Do this in remembrance of me" (Mt 26:26-27; 1 Cor 11:25).

7. Bread and wine are presented by the faithful and placed upon the altar by the priest. These are simple gifts, but they were foreshadowed in the Old Testament and chosen by Christ himself for the Eucharistic sacrifice. When these gifts of bread and wine are offered by the priest in the name of the Church to the Father in the great Eucharistic Prayer of thanksgiving, they are transformed by the Holy Spirit into the Body and Blood of the only-begotten Son of the Father. Finally, when the one bread is broken, "the unity of the faithful is expressed . . . [and through Communion they] receive from the one bread the Lord's body and blood in the same way the apostles received them from Christ's own hands."[16] Hence the import of the words of the hymn adapted from the *Didache*:

> As grain once scattered on the hillsides
> was in this broken bread made one
> so from all lands your church be gathered
> into your kingdom by your Son.[17]

---

15   CCC, no. 1382.

16   GIRM, no. 72(3).

17   F. Bland Tucker, trans., "Father, We Thank Thee, Who Hast Planted," a hymn adapted from the *Didache*, c. 110 (The Church Pension Fund, 1940).

Christ Himself Is Present in the Eucharistic Species

8. Christ is "truly, really, and substantially contained"[18] in Holy Communion. His presence is not momentary nor simply signified, but wholly and permanently real under each of the consecrated species of bread and wine.[19]

9. The Council of Trent teaches that "the true body and blood of our Lord, together with his soul and divinity, exist under the species of bread and wine. His body exists under the species of bread and his blood under the species of wine, according to the import of his words."[20]

10. The Church also teaches and believes that "immediately after the consecration the true body of our Lord and his true blood exist along with his soul and divinity under the form of bread and wine. The body is present under the form of bread and the blood under the form of wine, by virtue of the words [of Christ]. The same body, however, is under the form of wine and the blood under the form of bread, and the

---

18   Council of Trent, Session xiii (October 11, 1551), *Canones de ss. Eucharistiae sacramento*, can. 1 (DS 1651; TCT 728).

19   Cf. Council of Trent, Session xiii (October 11, 1551), *Decretum de ss. Eucharistiae sacramento*, cap. IV, *De transubstantione* (DS 1642; TCT 722): "Because Christ our Redeemer said that it was truly his body that he was offering under the species of bread (see Matthew 26:26ff.; Mark 14:22ff.; Luke 22:19ff.; 1 Corinthians 11:24ff.), it has always been the conviction of the Church, and this holy council now again declares it that, by the consecration of the bread and wine a change takes place in which the whole substance of bread is changed into the substance of the Body of Christ our Lord and the whole substance of the wine into the substance of his blood. This change the holy Catholic Church fittingly and properly names transubstantiation."

20   Council of Trent, Session xiii (October 11, 1551), *Decretum de ss. Eucharistiae sacramento*, cap. III, *De excellentia ss. Eucharistiae super reliqua sacramenta* (DS 1640; TCT 721).

soul under either form, by virtue of the natural link and concomitance by which the parts of Christ the Lord, who has now risen from the dead and will die no more, are mutually united."[21]

11. Since, however, by reason of the sign value, sharing in both Eucharistic species reflects more fully the sacred realities that the Liturgy signifies, the Church in her wisdom has made provisions in recent years so that more frequent Eucharistic participation from both the sacred host and the chalice of salvation might be made possible for the laity in the Latin Church.

Holy Communion as an Act of Faith

12. Christ's presence in the Eucharist challenges human understanding, logic, and ultimately reason. His presence cannot be known by the senses, but only through faith[22]—a faith that is continually deepened through that communion which takes place between the Lord and his faithful in the very act of the celebration of the Eucharist. Thus the Fathers frequently warned the faithful that by relying solely on their senses they would see only bread and wine. Rather, they exhorted the members of the Church to recall the word of Christ by whose power the bread and wine have been transformed into his own Body and Blood.[23]

13. The teaching of St. Cyril of Jerusalem assists the Church even today in understanding this great mystery:

---

21   Ibid. (DS 1640; Norman P. Tanner, ed., *Decrees of the Ecumenical Councils, Vol. 2: Trent to Vatican II* [London: Sheed & Ward, 1990], 695.)

22   Cf. CCC, no. 1381.

23   Cf. Paul VI, *Mysterium Fidei: On the Doctrine and Worship of the Eucharist* (September 3, 1965), no. 47 (in International Committee on English in the Liturgy, *Documents on the Liturgy, 1963-1979: Conciliar, Papal, and Curial Texts* [DOL] [1982] 176, no. 1192).

We have been instructed in these matters and filled with an unshakable faith that what seems to be bread is not bread, though it tastes like it, but the Body of Christ, and that what seems to be wine is not wine, though it tastes like it, but the Blood of Christ.[24]

14. The act of Communion, therefore, is also an act of faith. For when the minister says, "The Body of Christ" or "The Blood of Christ," the communicant's "Amen" is a profession in the presence of the saving Christ, body and blood, soul and divinity, who now gives life to the believer.

15. The communicant makes this act of faith in the total presence of the Lord Jesus Christ whether in Communion under one form or in Communion under both kinds. It should never be construed, therefore, that Communion under the form of bread alone or Communion under the form of wine alone is somehow an incomplete act or that Christ is not fully present to the communicant. The Church's unchanging teaching from the time of the Fathers through the ages—notably in the ecumenical councils of Lateran IV, Constance, Florence, Trent, and Vatican II—has witnessed to a constant unity of faith in the presence of Christ in both elements.[25] Clearly there are some pastoral circumstances that require Eucharistic sharing in one species only, such as when Communion is brought to the sick or when one is unable to receive either the Body of the Lord or the Precious Blood due to an illness. Even in the earliest days of the Church's life, when Communion under both species was the norm, there were always instances when the Eucharist was received under only the form of bread or wine. Those who received Holy Communion at home or who were sick would usually receive under only one species, as would the whole Church during

---

24   Ibid., no. 48 (DOL 176, no. 1193).
25   Cf. GIRM, no. 281.

the Good Friday Liturgy.[26] Thus, the Church has always taught the doctrine of concomitance, by which we know that under each species alone, the whole Christ is sacramentally present and we "receive all the fruit of Eucharistic grace."[27]

16. At the same time an appreciation for reception of "the whole Christ" through one species should not diminish in any way the fuller sign value of reception of Holy Communion under both kinds. For just as Christ offered his whole self, body and blood, as a sacrifice for our sins, so too is our reception of his Body and Blood under both kinds an especially fitting participation in his memorial of eternal life.

Holy Communion Under Both Kinds

17. From the first days of the Church's celebration of the Eucharist, Holy Communion consisted of the reception of both species in fulfillment of the Lord's command to "take and eat . . . take and drink." The distribution of Holy Communion to the faithful under both kinds was thus the norm for more than a millennium of Catholic liturgical practice.

18. The practice of Holy Communion under both kinds at Mass continued until the late eleventh century, when the custom of distributing the Eucharist to the faithful under the form of bread alone began to grow. By the twelfth century theologians such as Peter Cantor speak of Communion under one kind as a "custom" of the Church.[28] This practice spread until the Council of Constance in 1415 decreed that Holy Communion under the form of bread alone would be distributed to the faithful.

---

26 Cf. St. Cyprian, *De Lapsis*, 25, on Communion of infants and children; on Communion of the sick and dying, cf. *Statuta ecclesiae antiqua*, can. 76.

27 CCC, no. 1390.

28 Cf. Petrus Cantor, *Summa de Sacramentis et Animae Consiliis*, ed. J.-A. Dugauquier, *Analecta Medievalis Namurcensia*, vol. 4 (Louvain/Lille, 1954), I, 144.

19. In 1963, the Fathers of the Second Vatican Council authorized the extension of the faculty for Holy Communion under both kinds in *Sacrosanctum Concilium*:

> The dogmatic principles which were laid down by the Council of Trent remaining intact, Communion under both kinds may be granted when the bishops think fit, not only to clerics and religious, but also to the laity, in cases to be determined by the Apostolic See. . . .[29]

20. The Council's decision to restore Holy Communion under both kinds at the bishop's discretion took expression in the first edition of the *Missale Romanum* and enjoys an even more generous application in the third typical edition of the *Missale Romanum*:

> Holy Communion has a more complete form as a sign when it is received under both kinds. For in this manner of reception a fuller sign of the Eucharistic banquet shines forth. Moreover there is a clearer expression of that will by which the new and everlasting covenant is ratified in the blood of the Lord and of the relationship of the Eucharistic banquet to the eschatological banquet in the Father's kingdom.[30]

---

29 SC, no. 55.

30 GIRM, no. 281. The GIRM goes on to say, "For the faithful who take part in the rite or are present at it, pastors should take care to call to mind as appropriately as possible Catholic teaching according to the Council of Trent on the manner of Communion. Above all they should instruct the Christian faithful that, according to Catholic faith, Christ, whole and entire, as well as the true Sacrament are received under one kind only; that, therefore, as far as the effects are concerned, those who receive in this manner are not deprived of any grace necessary for salvation.

"Pastors are also to teach that the Church has the power in its stewardship of the sacraments, provided their substance remains intact, to make those rules and changes that, in view of the different conditions, times, and places, it decides to be in the interest of reverence for the sacraments or the well-being of the recipients" (no. 282).

The *General Instruction* further states that "at the same time the faithful should be guided toward a desire to take part more intensely in a sacred rite in which the sign of the Eucharistic meal stands out more explicitly."[31]

21. The extension of the faculty for the distribution of Holy Communion under both kinds does not represent a change in the Church's immemorial beliefs concerning the Holy Eucharist. Rather, today the Church finds it salutary to restore a practice, when appropriate, that for various reasons was not opportune when the Council of Trent was convened in 1545.[32] But with the passing of time, and under the guidance of the Holy Spirit, the reform of the Second Vatican Council has resulted in the restoration of a practice by which the faithful are again able to experience "a fuller sign of the Eucharistic banquet."[33]

31   Ibid., no. 282.

32   Cf. Council of Trent, Session xxi (July 16, 1562), *De doctrina de communione sub utraque specie et parvulorum* (DS 1725-1734; TCT 739-745).

33   Ibid.

PART II
Norms for the Distribution of Holy Communion Under Both Kinds

The Purpose of These Norms

22. In response to a provision of the *General Instruction of the Roman Missal*, the United States Conference of Catholic Bishops herein describes "the methods of distributing Holy Communion to the faithful under both kinds" and approves the following "norms, with the proper *recognitio* of the Apostolic See."[34] The purpose of these norms is to ensure the reverent and careful distribution of Holy Communion under both kinds.

When Communion Under Both Kinds May Be Given

23. The revised *Missale Romanum*, third typical edition, significantly expands those opportunities when Holy Communion may be offered under both kinds. In addition to those instances specified by individual ritual books, the *General Instruction* states that Communion under both kinds may be permitted as follows:

    a.   for priests who are not able to celebrate or concelebrate

    b.   for the deacon and others who perform some role at Mass

---

34   GIRM, no. 283.

c. for community members at their conventual Mass or what in some places is known as the "community" Mass, for seminarians, [and] for all who are on retreat or are participating in a spiritual or pastoral gathering[35]

24. The *General Instruction* then indicates that

the diocesan Bishop may lay down norms for the distribution of Communion under both kinds for his own diocese, which must be observed. . . . The diocesan Bishop also has the faculty to allow Communion under both kinds, whenever it seems appropriate to the priest to whom charge of a given community has been entrusted as [its] own pastor, provided that the faithful have been well instructed and there is no danger of the profanation of the Sacrament or that the rite would be difficult to carry out on account of the number of participants or for some other reason.[36]

In practice, the need to avoid obscuring the role of the priest and the deacon as the ordinary ministers of Holy Communion by an excessive use of extraordinary ministers might in some circumstances constitute a reason either for limiting the distribution of Holy Communion under both species or for using intinction instead of distributing the Precious Blood from the chalice.

Norms established by the diocesan bishop must be observed wherever the Eucharist is celebrated in the diocese, "even in the churches of religious orders and in celebrations with small groups."[37]

---

35   Ibid.

36   Ibid.

37   Ibid.

Catechesis for Receiving the Body and Blood of the Lord

25. When Communion under both kinds is first introduced by the diocesan bishop and also whenever the opportunity for instruction is present, the faithful should be properly catechized on the following matters in the light of the teaching and directives of the *General Instruction*:

a. the ecclesial nature of the Eucharist as the common possession of the whole Church;

b. the Eucharist as the memorial of Christ's sacrifice, his death and resurrection, and as the sacred banquet;

c. the real presence of Christ in the Eucharistic elements, whole and entire—in each element of consecrated bread and wine (the doctrine of concomitance);

d. the kinds of reverence due at all times to the sacrament, whether within the Eucharistic Liturgy or outside the celebration;[38] and

e. the role that ordinary and, if necessary, extraordinary ministers of the Eucharist are assigned in the Eucharistic assembly

The Minister of Holy Communion

26. By virtue of his sacred ordination, the bishop or priest offers the sacrifice in the person of Christ, the Head of the Church. He receives gifts of bread and wine from the faithful, offers the sacrifice to God, and returns to them the very Body and Blood of Christ, as from the hands of Christ himself.[39] Thus bishops and priests are considered the ordinary ministers of Holy Communion. In addition, the deacon who assists the bishop or priest in distributing Communion is an ordinary minister of Holy Communion. When the Eucharist is distributed under both forms, "the deacon ministers the chalice."[40]

---

38 Cf. Congregation of Rites, *Eucharisticum Mysterium: On Worship of the Eucharist* [EM] (May 25, 1967), part I, "General Principles to Be Given Prominence in Catechizing the People on the Eucharistic Mystery" (DOL 179, nos. 1234-1244).

39 Cf. GIRM, no. 93.

40 GIRM, no. 182.

27. In every celebration of the Eucharist there should be a sufficient number of ministers for Holy Communion so that it can be distributed in an orderly and reverent manner. Bishops, priests, and deacons distribute Holy Communion by virtue of their office as ordinary ministers of the Body and Blood of the Lord.[41]

Extraordinary Ministers of Holy Communion

28. When the size of the congregation or the incapacity of the bishop, priest, or deacon requires it, the celebrant may be assisted by other bishops, priests, or deacons.[42] If such ordinary ministers of Holy Communion are not present, "the priest may call upon extraordinary ministers to assist him, i.e., formally instituted acolytes or even some of the faithful who have been commissioned according to the prescribed rite. In case of necessity, the priest may also commission suitable members of the faithful for the occasion."[43] Extraordinary ministers of Holy Communion should receive sufficient spiritual, theological, and practical preparation to fulfill their role with knowledge and reverence. When recourse is had to extraordinary ministers of Holy Communion, especially in the distribution of Holy Communion under both kinds, their number should not be increased beyond what is required for the orderly and reverent distribution of the Body and Blood of the Lord. In all matters, such extraordinary ministers of Holy Communion should follow the guidance of the diocesan bishop.

Reverence

29. All ministers of Holy Communion should show the greatest reverence for the Most Holy Eucharist by their demeanor, their attire, and the manner in which they handle the consecrated bread or wine.

---

41 Cf. GIRM, no. 108.

42 Cf. GIRM, no. 162.

43 GIRM, no. 162. Cf. also Sacred Congregation for the Discipline of the Sacraments, *Immensae Caritatis: Instruction on Facilitating Reception of Communion in Certain Circumstances*, section 1.I.c (DOL 264, no. 2075).

Should there be any mishap—as when, for example, the consecrated wine is spilled from the chalice—then the affected "area . . . should be washed and the water poured into the sacrarium."[44]

Planning

30. When Holy Communion is to be distributed under both species, careful planning should be undertaken so that:

- enough bread and wine are made ready for the communication of the faithful at each Mass.[45] As a general rule, Holy Communion is given from hosts consecrated at the same Mass and not from those reserved in the tabernacle. Precious Blood may not be reserved at one Mass for use at another;[46] and
- a suitable number of ministers of Holy Communion are provided at each Mass. For Communion from the chalice, it is desirable that there be generally two ministers of the Precious Blood for each minister of the Body of Christ, lest the liturgical celebration be unduly prolonged.

31. Even when Communion will be ministered in the form of bread alone to the congregation, care should be taken that sufficient amounts

---

44 GIRM, no. 280.

45 Cf. EM, no. 31 (DOL 179, no. 1260): "The faithful share more fully in the celebration of the eucharist through sacramental communion. It is strongly recommended that they should receive it as a rule in the Mass itself and at that point in the celebration which is prescribed by the rite, that is, right after the communion of the priest celebrant.

"In order that the communion may stand out more clearly even through signs as a participation in the sacrifice actually being celebrated, steps should be taken that enable the faithful to receive hosts consecrated at that Mass."

46 Cf. GIRM, no. 284b: "Whatever happens to remain of the Blood [after the distribution of Holy Communion] is consumed at the altar by the priest or deacon or instituted acolyte who ministered the chalice. . . ."

of the elements are consecrated so that the Precious Blood may be distributed to all concelebrating priests.

Preparations

32. Before Mass begins, wine and hosts should be provided in vessels of appropriate size and number. The presence on the altar of a single chalice and one large paten can signify the one bread and one chalice by which we are gathered "into the one Body of Christ, a living sacrifice of praise."[47] When this is not possible, care should be taken that the number of vessels should not exceed the need.

33. The unity of all in the one bread will be better expressed when the bread to be broken is of sufficient size that at least some of the faithful are able to receive a piece broken from it. When the number of the faithful is great, however, a single large bread may be used for the breaking of the bread with small breads provided for the rest of the faithful.[48]

34. Sacred vessels, which "hold a place of honor," should be of noble materials, appropriate to their use, and in conformity to the requirements of liturgical law, as specified in the *General Instruction of the Roman Missal*, nos. 327-332.

35. Before being used, vessels for the celebration must be blessed by the bishop or priest according to the *Rite of Blessing a Chalice and Paten*.[49]

At the Preparation of the Gifts

36. The altar is prepared with corporal, purificator, *Missal*, and chalice (unless the chalice is prepared at a side table) by the deacon and servers. The gifts of bread and wine are brought forward by the faithful and received by the priest or deacon at a convenient place.[50]

---

47 *Sacramentary*, Eucharistic Prayer IV.
48 Cf. GIRM, no. 321.
49 Cf. GIRM, no. 333.
50 Cf. ibid., no. 73.

At the Breaking of the Bread

37. As the *Agnus Dei* or *Lamb of God* is begun, the bishop or priest alone, or with the assistance of the deacon, and if necessary of concelebrating priests, breaks the Eucharistic bread.

Other empty chalices and ciboria or patens are then brought to the altar if this is necessary. The deacon or priest places the consecrated bread in several ciboria or patens and, if necessary, pours the Precious Blood into enough additional chalices as are required for the distribution of Holy Communion. If it is not possible to accomplish this distribution in a reasonable time, the celebrant may call upon the assistance of other deacons or concelebrating priests. This action is usually carried out at the altar, so that the sharing of all from the one cup is signified; in the case of large assemblies, it may be done at the side table within the sanctuary (*presbyterium*).

38. If extraordinary ministers of Holy Communion are required by pastoral need, they approach the altar as the priest receives Communion. After the priest has concluded his own Communion, he distributes Communion to the extraordinary ministers, assisted by the deacon, and then hands the sacred vessels to them for distribution of Holy Communion to the people.

39. All receive Holy Communion in the manner described by the *General Instruction to the Roman Missal*, whether priest concelebrants (cf. GIRM, nos. 159, 242, 243, 246), deacons (cf. GIRM, nos. 182, 244, 246), or extraordinary ministers of Holy Communion (cf. GIRM, no. 284). Neither deacons nor lay ministers may ever receive Holy Communion in the manner of a concelebrating priest. The practice of extraordinary ministers of Holy Communion waiting to receive Holy Communion until after the distribution of Holy Communion is not in accord with liturgical law.

40. After all Eucharistic ministers have received Communion, the bishop or priest celebrant reverently hands vessels containing the Body or the Blood of the Lord to the deacons or extraordinary ministers who will assist with the distribution of Holy Communion. The deacon may assist the priest in handing the vessels containing the Body and Blood of the Lord to the extraordinary ministers of Holy Communion.

Distribution of the Body and Blood of the Lord

41. Holy Communion under the form of bread is offered to the communicant with the words "The Body of Christ." The communicant may choose whether to receive the Body of Christ in the hand or on the tongue. When receiving in the hand, the communicant should be guided by the words of St. Cyril of Jerusalem: "When you approach, take care not to do so with your hand stretched out and your fingers open or apart, but rather place your left hand as a throne beneath your right, as befits one who is about to receive the King. Then receive him, taking care that nothing is lost."[51]

42. Among the ways of ministering the Precious Blood as prescribed by the *General Instruction of the Roman Missal*, Communion from the chalice is generally the preferred form in the Latin Church, provided that it can be carried out properly according to the norms and without any risk of even apparent irreverence toward the Blood of Christ.[52]

43. The chalice is offered to the communicant with the words "The Blood of Christ," to which the communicant responds, "Amen."

---

51 Cat. Myst. V, 21-22.

52 Cf. Sacred Congregation for Divine Worship, *Sacramentali Communione: Instruction Extending the Practice of Communion Under Both Kinds* (June 29, 1970), no. 6 (DOL 270, no. 2115).

44. The chalice may never be left on the altar or another place to be picked up by the communicant for self-communication (except in the case of concelebrating bishops or priests), nor may the chalice be passed from one communicant to another. There shall always be a minister of the chalice.

45. After each communicant has received the Blood of Christ, the minister carefully wipes both sides of the rim of the chalice with a purificator. This action is a matter of both reverence and hygiene. For the same reason, the minister turns the chalice slightly after each communicant has received the Precious Blood.

46. It is the choice of the communicant, not the minister, to receive from the chalice.

47. Children are encouraged to receive Communion under both kinds provided that they are properly instructed and that they are old enough to receive from the chalice.

Other Forms of Distribution of the Precious Blood
48. Distribution of the Precious Blood by a spoon or through a straw is not customary in the Latin dioceses of the United States of America.

49. Holy Communion may be distributed by intinction in the following manner: "the communicant, while holding the paten under the chin, approaches the priest who holds the vessel with the hosts and at whose side stands a minister holding the chalice. The priest takes the host, intincts the particle into the chalice and, showing it, says: 'The Body and Blood of Christ.' The communicant responds, 'Amen,' and receives the Sacrament on the tongue from the priest. Afterwards, the communicant returns to his or her place."[53]

---

53   GIRM, no. 287.

50. The communicant, including the extraordinary minister, is never allowed to self-communicate, even by means of intinction. Communion under either form, bread or wine, must always be given by an ordinary or extraordinary minister of Holy Communion.

Purification of Sacred Vessels

51. After Communion the consecrated bread that remains is to be reserved in the tabernacle. Care should be taken with any fragments remaining on the corporal or in the sacred vessels. The deacon returns to the altar with the priest and collects and consumes any remaining fragments.

52. When more of the Precious Blood remains than was necessary for Communion, and if not consumed by the bishop or priest celebrant, "the deacon immediately and reverently consumes at the altar all of the Blood of Christ which remains; he may be assisted, if needs dictate, by other deacons and priests."[54] When there are extraordinary ministers of Holy Communion, they may consume what remains of the Precious Blood from their chalice of distribution with permission of the diocesan bishop.

53. The chalice and other vessels may be taken to a side table, where they are cleansed and arranged in the usual way. Other sacred vessels that held the Precious Blood are purified in the same way as chalices. Provided the remaining consecrated bread has been consumed or reserved and the remaining Precious Blood has been consumed, "it is permissible to leave the vessels . . . suitably covered and at a side table on a corporal, to be cleansed immediately after Mass following the dismissal of the people."[55]

---

54   GIRM, no. 182.
55   GIRM, no. 183.

54. The Precious Blood may not be reserved, except for giving Communion to someone who is sick. Only sick people who are unable to receive Communion under the form of bread may receive it under the form of wine alone at the discretion of the priest. If not consecrated at a Mass in the presence of the sick person, the Blood of the Lord is kept in a properly covered vessel and is placed in the tabernacle after Communion. The Precious Blood should be carried to the sick in a vessel that is closed in such a way as to eliminate all danger of spilling. If some of the Precious Blood remains after the sick person has received Communion, it should be consumed by the minister, who should also see to it that the vessel is properly purified.

55. The reverence due to the Precious Blood of the Lord demands that it be fully consumed after Communion is completed and never be poured into the ground or the sacrarium.

CONCLUSION

56. The norms and directives established by the Church for the celebration of any liturgical rite always have as their immediate goal the proper and careful celebration of those rites. However, such directives also have as their purpose the fostering of celebrations that glorify God and deepen the faith, hope, and charity of the participants in liturgical worship. The ordered preparation and celebration of the Mass, and of Holy Communion in particular, should always profoundly affect the faith of communicants in all its aspects and dimensions. In the case of the distribution of Holy Communion under both kinds, Christian faith in the real presence of Christ in the Holy Eucharist can only be renewed and deepened in the life of the faithful by this esteemed practice.

57. In all other matters pertaining to the Rite of Communion under both kinds, the directives of the *General Instruction*, nos. 281-287, are to be consulted.

559